Fairy Women

from the Portuguese

Book of Lineages of Count Dom Pedro

POLITICS, MYSTICISM, AND MAGIC

Fairy Women from the Portuguese
Book of Lineages of Count Dom Pedro:
Politics, Mysticism, and Magic
Copyright © 2024 José Leitão
Cover design & illustrataion © S. Aldarnay

ISBN 978-1-915933-07-2 (Hardcover)
ISBN 978-1-915933-65-2 (Softcover)

A catalogue for this title is available from the
British Library.
10 9 8 7 6 5 4 3 2 1

Published in 2024 Papaveria Press
An imprint of Hadean Press Limited
West Yorkshire England
www.hadeanpress.com

fct Fundação
para a Ciência
e a Tecnologia

REPÚBLICA
PORTUGUESA

C H S C CENTRO DE HISTÓRIA
DA SOCIEDADE
E DA CULTURA

UIDB/00311/2020

Fairy Women

from the Portuguese

Book of Lineages of Count Dom Pedro

POLITICS, MYSTICISM, AND MAGIC

José Leitão

Papaveria Press
Fairylore Series

Contents

Fairy Women from the Portuguese
Book of Lineages of Count Dom Pedro

Among the mythical and folkloric pantheons of Iberia, two legends stand out due to their ancestry and durability. Situated within the wider world of Iberian *fadas*, *hadas*, *janas*, *xanas* and *mouras*, these stories are unique, be it due to their historical contexts or their characters. Both come into preeminence in the fourteenth century, and not as expressions of local folk culture, but rather from a literary compilation: the *Livro das Linhagens do Conde Dom Pedro*, or *the Book of Lineages of Count Dom Pedro*. These are the tales of the melusinian fairy women Dama do Pé-de-Cabra and Dona Marinha.

Count Dom Pedro, or Pedro Afonso, third Count of Barcelos (1287-1354), was the first-born 'natural' son of King Denis of Portugal, the Farmer- or Poet-King (1261-1325). Like his father, he was an accomplished poet and troubadour whose name can be found on several of the most important cultural productions

of the Portuguese medieval period. Pedro
Afonso was also a skilled diplomat, having
been known to accompany Denis and his
legitimate wife, Saint Elizabeth Queen of
Portugal,[1] across the Iberian Peninsula as a
mediator of political and military disputes.[2]

Pedro's skills would eventually be used
in his own home kingdom, as Denis'
centralizing policies gave rise to severe
tensions between the Crown and the
nobility. In this context, Pedro Afonso was
given various benefits by his father as a
way of keeping him close and favorable to
the king's faction against the nobles. Thus,
while the nobility was gathering around
Pedro's half-brother, the Crown-prince and
future King Afonso IV, Pedro was made the
Count of Barcelos and *alferez-mor* of the
kingdom (chief-standard-bearer, the head
of the kingdom's military).[3] Eventually,
Pedro Afonso would himself demonstrate

---

1 Pedro Afonso was born before the marriage
of Denis and Elizabeth, so it was probably not
as awkward as it might seem.

2 PIZARRO – *D. Dinis*, p. 119-20.

3 PIZARRO – *D. Dinis*, p. 240.

sympathy for the nobles' cause, and was
exiled by his father to the Castilian court of
Alfonso IX between 1317 and 1322, where
he immersed himself in Castilian literature
and culture.[4]

The political tension between the lords
and the Crown eventually resulted in a
civil war between Denis and the Crown-
prince, at the conclusion of which Pedro
Afonso returned to his home kingdom to
mediate the conflict between his father and
half-brother together with Queen Saint
Elizabeth, achieving a somewhat shaky
peace in the year of 1324.[5] After the death
of Denis the following year, Pedro further
brought his literary skills to the conciliation
table by initiating the composition of a
book of lineages inspired by the chronicles
and records he had studied in Castile.
As pointed out by Luís Krus, medieval
books of lineages served very concrete
political purposes. Such books tended
to emerge during periods of Crown or
Papal encroachment upon local power by

4 PIZARRO – *D. Dinis*, p. 182, 240.
5 PIZARRO – *D. Dinis*, p. 193-4.

bringing forward narratives of familial and genealogical authority and glory capable of matching or even obfuscating that of the king or a noble rival.[6] Pedro Afonso's intention with his *Book* is explicitly stated as that of "love and friendship among the nobles of Spain".[7] In this way he offered the contending noble houses a conciliatory and legitimizing narrative of power and authority bound to the genealogical line of Portuguese kings which would insure their respectability and rights in the eyes of the Crown.[8] Not long after this, Pedro would also compose the *Crónica Geral de Espanha de 1344 (General Chronicle of Spain of 1344)*, where he would portray his father as a good, generous, and merciful king, blessed by God and the object of miracles and

6 KRUS – 'A Morte das Fadas,' p. 3-5.

7 'amor e amizade antre os nobres fidallgos da espanha,' in ANTT, Livros de Linhagens, Nobiliário de Espanha Escrito pelo Senhor Conde D. Pedro, fol.1v; In this context, 'Spain'/'Espanha' refers to Iberia, as Spain was not a country or kingdom until 1714.

8 FERREIRA – «Amor e Amizade Antre os Nobres Fidalgos de Espanha», p. 97.

divine favor, second only to King Henry, the first Portuguese monarch:[9] literary balms for the wounds of war.

---

9 PIZARRO – *D. Dinis*, p. 18, 202.

Cover page of Pedro Afonso's *Book of Lineages*. Sixteenth century edition currently in the custody of the Arquivo Nacional da Torre do Tombo (1693 binding).

Opening page of Pedro Afonso's *Book of Lineages*. Sixteenth century edition currently in the custody of the Arquivo Nacional da Torre do Tombo (1693 binding).

The production of the *Book of Lineages
of Count Dom Pedro* is believed to have oc-
curred between 1340 and 1344, with Pedro
being known to have used as his sources the
thirteenth century Cistercian *Liber Regum*,
or *Chronicon Villarense* and the *Crónica Gale-
go-Portuguesa de Espanha e Portugal*, a currently
unknown book only mentioned in secondary sources.[10] In the Portuguese kingdom
Pedro Afonso's work was the third of its
kind, being preceded by what is usually referred to as the *Livro Velho de Linhagens*, the
Old Book of Lineages, believed to have been
composed around the 1270s in the context of the power-centralizing policies of
King Afonso III, Denis' father (of which
no complete copy remains), and the *Livro
do Deão*, the *Dean's Book*, from 1337-1340.[11]

---

10 KRUS – 'A Morte das Fadas,' p. 14;
MATTOSO – *Narrativas dos Livros de Linhagens*,
p. 19, 21-2.

11 FERREIRA – «Amor e Amizade Antre os
Nobres Fidalgos de Espanha», p. 4; A critical
edition of the known content of these two
earlier *Books of Lineages* can be consulted in
PIEL and MATTOSO – 'Livros Velhos de
Linhagens'.

While building upon the previously established narrative lines of the *Livro Velho* and
the *Livro do Deão*, this new book of lineages
had less localized preoccupations; dealing
with several lineages from the entire Iberian Peninsula, it brought into play a number
of new genealogical foundation narratives
that, while likely existing in previous oral
forms or in currently unknown literary
versions, were new to the book of lineages
tradition.[12] These are the melusinian foundation tales of the Haros of Biscay and the
Marinhos of Galicia, stories which have
come to be known as the *Dama do Pé-de-
Cabra* (Lady Goat-Foot) and *Dona Marinha*
(Lady of the Sea).

Such supernatural foundation tales, by
the fourteenth century, were fairly common outside of Iberia, with their literary
footprint being particularly noticeable between 1170 and 1210 and culminating in
the tale which names the entire genre, that
of the fairy Melusine, whose name is only
established in the late fourteenth century

12 PRIETO LASA – *Las Leyendas de los Señores
de Vizcaya*, p. 26.

and takes its most widespread form in the narrative of the *Roman de Mélusine* by Jean d'Arras.[13] In its basic form, this tale narrates the encounter of a local lord with a fairy or land-bound non-human entity who establishes a pact with him in the form of marriage and the guarantee of powerful descendants in exchange for the following of a strict taboo. This taboo, which is eventually broken, results in the fairy-woman abandoning her husband, leaving behind their children who, though occasionally described as somewhat monstrous, establish one or several noble lines of repute and power. In the particular case of Melusine, those were the Houses of Luxemburg, Anjou, Plantagenet, and Lusignan.

The purpose of such a mythical or fantastic genealogical narrative is not dissimilar from that of a 'regular' lineage narrative, as these can also be understood as establishing legitimacy through a form

13 KRUS – 'A Morte das Fadas,' p. 7; See LE GOFF – 'Mélusine Maternelle et Défricheuse'; LECAUTEUX – 'La Structure des Légendes Mélusiniennes'.

of inherent authority which is not subject to the standard fief-vassal code nor based on human contracts, deals, or favors, thereby challenging Christianity's monopoly on power dispensation.[14] Such supernatural lineages are thus seen as capable of justifying sudden and unexplainable rises to and falls from power and an irreducible relation of a family to a particular piece of land or dominion which is thus subtracted from kingly authority. Still, such narratives are double-edged swords, as they can also be used or created by a lord's political rivals in order to portray their ancestors as participants in diabolical pacts and initiators of a tainted lineage.[15] This is obviously not an exclusively Iberian issue, and even the d'Arras Melusine tale is itself a narrative meant to reenforce the claim of the Duke of Berry, d'Arras' patron, to Poitou and Lusignan.[16]

---

14 KRUS – 'A Morte das Fadas,' p. 10.

15 KRUS – 'A Morte das Fadas,' p. 11-12.

16 URBAN, KEMMIS and ELMES – 'Introduction,' p. 5

*

Looking at the two Portuguese books of
lineages' melusinian-tales individually, the
first of these, both in chronological terms
and current influence and distribution, is
usually referred to in academic literature as
the *Dama de Vizcaya* or the *Dama de los Haro*
(Lady of Biscay or Lady of the Haros),
but is otherwise popularly known by the
historically anachronistic name of *Dama do
Pé-de-Cabra* (Lady Goat-Foot).[17] Originating
in Biscay, a border region between the
medieval kingdoms of Castile and Navarre,
this is a power-legitimizing narrative of the
Haro family who were connected to the
Portuguese royal lineage by Queen Mécia
Lopes de Haro, wife of King Sancho II,
Pedro Afonso's great grandfather. Biscay
was a politically complex territory in
which its lords constantly negotiated
their affiliations and fealties between the
aforementioned kingdoms of Castile and
Navarre, generating ideal opportunities

---

17 PRIETO LASA – *Las Leyendas de los Señores
de Vizcaya*, p. 16.

for the strengthening of lordship rights.[18]
In this context, it is likely that the legend
of Lady Goat-Foot can be traced to
the eleventh century, making it the first
known instance of a melusinian-tale in
the Iberian Peninsula. The medievalist
Luís Krus suggests that its original author
was possibly the troubadour Rigaut de
Berbezilh who was known to have spent
a considerable amount of time in the
court of Diego López II of Haro, with
there being various possible moments
of retelling and rewriting the tale in
the subsequent decades.[19] One of these
moments likely happened during the early
thirteenth-century conflict between Diogo
Lopes of Haro and the Castilian King
Alfonso VIII (1201-1205), in which Diogo
Lopes broke his vassalage to Castile and
turned towards Navarre.[20] Accompanying
this political move was the composition

18 KRUS – 'A Morte das Fadas,' p. 21.

19 KRUS – 'A Morte das Fadas,' p. 38; KRUS
– *A Concepção Nobiliárquica do Espaço Ibérico*, p.
469.

20 KRUS – 'A Morte das Fadas,' p. 30.

of a new genealogical narrative opposed
to Castilian power and dominance. This
narrative, as presented in Pedro Afonso's
Book of Lineages, traces the genealogy of the
Biscayan lords to the mythological Froom,
the supposed banished brother of the
King of England, and thus related to the
genealogy of King Arthur (which Pedro
Afonso also included in his *Book of Lineages*;
the Arthurian theme is also common in
the tales of Melusine proper). Froom,
being able to repel the encroachment of
the Asturian Count Moninho, Moniño or
Munio upon the rights of the Biscayans,
is acclaimed as lord of the land by the
locals in the aftermath of the Battle of
Arrigorriaga, with his descendants later
wedding the land itself, personified by the
fairy Goat-Foot.[21]

The narrative around Goat-Foot
itself, while being fitted to the melusinian
model in the eleventh century, was likely

21 MATTOSO – *Narrativas dos Livros de Linhagens*,
p. 38-9, 24-6; URBAN, KEMMIS and ELMES
– 'Introduction,' p. 5; KRUS – 'A Morte das
Fadas,' p. 25-6; MONREAL ZIA, DOUGLASS
and WHITE – *The Old Law of Bizkaia*, p. 70.

constructed from various local notions and folkloric concepts, probably circulating in oral form around Biscay and associated with Basque-specific ideas of land authority and dominion. Overall, Goat-Foot stands as a rather irreverent form of the Melusine story, with her physical description marking her as considerably distinct from other fairy-wives of the genre: her most noticeable non-human aspect is a single cloven foot, like that of a goat, rather than any serpent-like characteristics or aquatic associations. Furthermore, the nature of Goat-Foot's taboo, that of her husband not being allowed to bless himself, likely places this narrative closer to Walter Map's 'Henno cum Dentibus', Henno-with-the-Teeth, included in his *De Nugis Curialium*, and Gervase of Tilbury's tale of Count Raymond from *Otia Imperialia*, both from the thirteenth century.[22] Furthermore, Goat-Foot's particular physical aspect, from a Basque perspective, immediately associates her with the deity of Mari, or,

---

22 BAIN – 'The Tail of Melusine,' p. 21

alternatively, indicates her as a Basque *lamia* (pl. *lamiak*, *laminak* or *lamiñak*).

Lamiak are themselves complex cultural constructs, with possible connections to classical Greek and Roman lamias. However and whenever their introduction to the Basque Country happened, this word became associated with a type of spirit under the dominion of Mari, the central Basque deity, often described as having fish tails in coastal regions, but otherwise mentioned as beautiful women with chicken, duck, or goat feet, with noticeable representation in Northeastern Biscay.[23]

Regarding Mari herself, such is equally a complex topic to approach, with possible non-Indo-European roots but equally constructed from Christian and medieval elements. Invariably, Mari is associated

---

23 ARANZADI – *Milenarismo Vasco*, p. 360; ARANZADI – 'Mari, Melusina y los Origenes Miticos de los Señores de Vizcaya', p. 6; CONSTANZA CERUTI – 'Montañas Sagradas en el País Vasco e su Mitologia', p. 39; CARO BAROJA – *Algunos Mitos Españoles*, p. 43-4.

with the underground; the earth, from a Basque perspective, is a flat surface, under which rests a paradise-like place, flowing with milk and filled with treasure, which the souls of the ancestors and all mythical figures inhabit. Connections to this location, and to Mari, can be found in caves in particular and specific mountains in the Basque Country, between which Mari travels in a variety of forms, such as several atmospheric events including gusts of wind, a white cloud, the rainbow, a ball of fire or a shooting star. She is also able to take several animal forms such as ravens, horses, and particularly that of a male goat, or can appear as a beautiful woman surrounded by fire and frequently with bird or goat feet.[24] On each of her mountains Mari has her own toponymical title, such as *Mari de Aralar*, *Santa de la Cueva*, *Señorita de Lizárraga*, *Señora de Numo* or *Dama del Amboto*, all distinct and the same.[25]

---

24 ARANZADI – *Milenarismo Vasco*, p. 338-9.

25 CONSTANZA CERUTI – 'Montañas Sagradas en el País Vasco e su Mitologia', p. 36

Likely stemming from her non-Indo-European roots, the uncommon collection of symbols, names, and manifestations connected with Mari are a challenge to grasp and interpret, and they can frequently give rise to contemporary association-games leading to ample academic pitfalls. An example of this, I believe, can be seen in some propositions by the scholar and poet Jon Juristi of the relationship between Mari and Maria de Padilla. The name of Maria de Padilla should be firstly noted as referring to the historical mistress of Peter I of Castile (1334-1369), who, according to subsequent literary elaborations, was said to have made this monarch abandon his legitimate wife, Queen Blanca de Borbón (1339-1361), and was also assumed to be responsible for her death. Within an uncertain timeframe, this name becomes associated with magic and magical practice, becoming a particularly relevant intermediary spirit in Iberian urban folk magic in the early modern period.[26]

---

26 PAIVA – *Bruxaria e Superstição*, p. 102.

Besides such folk magic practices, references to Maria de Padilla can also be found in many literary sources, with her occasionally being described as roaming the skies or riding in a coach of fire, such as by the Sevillian poet and historian Rodrigo Caro (1573-1647).[27] Relating Mari with Maria de Padilla based on these perfunctory descriptions, while tempting, cannot be taken at face value given the irreducible geographical and cultural distance between the folkloric Basque Mari and such learned or literary mentions of Maria de Padilla. And while Maria de Padilla does become a relevant and widespread folk figure in the early modern period, of the several dozens of references found of her in Iberian and South American inquisitorial documentation, none of them seems to describe her as riding in a chariot of fire or associate her with any other of the common Mari symbols. She is rather associated with the urban streets, once

---

27 JUARISTI – 'Los Mitos de Origen en la Génesis de las Identidades Nacionales', p. 213; CARO – *Días Geniales ó Lúdicros*, p. 302.

being referred to in a Lisbon Inquisition trial as the *Senhora de la Calhe* (Lady/Mistress of the street).[28] Still, should such a proposal be accepted for 'creative' purposes, this would consequently also relate Mari and Goat-Foot with the Brazilian Quimbanda *Pomba Giras*, an hypotheses given further flair by the description of several *Pomba Giras* and *Exus* as having one single cloven foot.

*

The tale of Dona Marinha, while thematically closer to the standard Melusine legend, radically breaks the melusinian-tale structure by the non-inclusion of the pact and taboo established between the fairy woman and her nobleman husband. Furthermore, this is likely a later and direct adaptation of the Goat-Foot narrative, albeit much simpler and streamlined. Krus

---

28 ANTT, Tribunal do Santo Ofício, Inquisição de Lisboa, Processos, nº5605, fol.92v; I know you're brilliant Juristi, and that you love your people and your culture, but you can't have it all.

suggests this was likely composed between 1284 and 1286 by Paio Gomes Charinho, a Castilian admiral and troubadour, descended through his mother's side from the Galician Marinhos.[29]

Behind this composition is probably a loss of favor Charinho suffered in the court of Sancho IV of Castile in favor of Lope Dias de Haro. Upon being forced to return to Galicia, Paio Gomes is thought to have composed the Dona Marinha tale explicitly based on the Goat-Foot tale so as to give his family a supernatural authority similar to that of his rival. While the Goat-Foot tale, following the standard melusinian-theme, has her abandon her husband upon his breaking of her fairy taboo (in this case, blessing himself), the Dona Marinha story presents a 'happy ending', with its protagonist being able to overcome his fairy-bride's non-human aspect and christianize her. In this way Paio Gomes portrayed his ancestors as superior to those of Haro's by having them being

29 KRUS – *A Concepção Nobiliárquica do Espaço Ibérico*, p. 469.

able to hold on to their supernatural wife.[30]

This thesis is, however, not universally accepted, with the scholar Isabel Cardigos suggesting a possible connection between Dona Marinha and the 'Sicilian Melusine' mentioned in one of the Cistercian Geoffrey of Auxerre's sermons from the *Super Apocalypsim*, which follows the standard melusinian mold (closer to the Goat-Foot tale) and which was disseminated with some frequency until the fifteenth century by Hélinand de Froidmont, Vicente de Beauvais, or Ulrich Molitor.[31] Another possible origin for some of the more unique elements in the Dona Marinha tale, as also proposed by Cardigos, is the story of Julnar the Sea-Born of the *Alf Laylah wa-Laylah*, the *One Thousand and One Nights*, which might itself be the origin of the Auxerre sermon.[32]

---

30 KRUS – *A Concepção Nobiliárquica do Espaço Ibérico*, p. 469-70.

31 CARDIGOS – «Dona Marinha», p. 75, 77-8; PRIETO LASA – *Las Leyendas de los Señores de Vizcaya*, p. 169-70.

32 CARDIGOS – «Dona Marinha», p. 79-80.

Be that as it may, it seems the Dona Marinha tale was never taken particularly seriously among the Galician Marinhos/Mariños, with the earliest local written version dating from the fifteenth century, making Pedro Afonso's *Book of Lineages* the earliest known record of the story.[33] Even examining later non-Portuguese retellings of the Marinho/Mariño lineages offers slightly distinct narratives, such as that found in Diego Hernández de Mendoza's *Nobiliario de Casas y Linages, Armas y Apellidos y sus Denominaciones y Derivaciones* (also from the fifteenth century), where, while the Marinho line is still founded by the child of a sea woman, she is not given a personal name.[34] Much more radical is the report found in Antonio Torquemada's *Iardin de Flores Cvriosas* (1570), which entirely removes Dona Marinha from the tale, making the supernatural sire of the Marinho bloodline

---

33 TENREIRO BERMÚDEZ – 'A Lenda Melusínica no Folclore Galego,' p. 265-6.

34 BNE, MSS/18244 V.1, fol.216r-217r; PRIETO LASA – *Las Leyendas de los Señores de Vizcaya*, p. 138.

a male triton (a fish man) who sexually attacked an unnamed Galician woman.[35] Overall, what consecrates the Dona Marinha story in Portugal was its adoption by several Marinhos who settled in the Portuguese kingdom during the reign of Afonso III. Such low-nobility Galician knights were usually looked-down upon by Portuguese aristocracy, and such was likely a way for the Portuguese Marinhos to claim a powerful, autonomous, and prestigious ancestry in their new home, with the addition of this narrative to Pedro Afonso's *Book of Lineages* securing their position in the kingdom.[36]

---

35 TORQUEMADA – *Iardin de Flores Cvriosas*, p. 100-1.

36 KRUS – *A Concepção Nobiliárquica do Espaço Ibérico*, p. 470.

FOLLOWING PAGE: DETAIL OF BARTOLOMEO
PARETO'S 1455 MAP OF EUROPE SHOWING
THE RELATIVE POSITIONS OF NAVARRE, BISCAY,
CASTILE, GALICIA, AND PORTUGAL.

*

The propagation of the Goat-Foot and
Dona Marinha tales from the medieval
until the contemporary period is a story
unto itself. Among the two, as already
stated, the Goat-Foot tale tends to be the
most popular, with its presence being
common in subsequent Portuguese and
Castilian versions of Pedro Afonso's *Book
of Lineages*, be it in full or truncated form.
Examples of these incomplete versions are
those present in Juan Bautista Labaña's[37]
1640 Rome edition of the *Book of Lineages*
and its Castilian translation by Manuel de
Faria y Sousa, published in 1646 in Madrid;
these versions completely exclude the Dona
Marinha tale from their pages.[38] Other
authors and learned authorities during
the modern period offer several forms or

---

37 Also referred to as Juan Bautista Lavaña or
João Baptista Lavanha, Chief-cosmographer
of the Kingdom of Portugal and master at the
Madrid Academy of Mathematics, nominated
by Philip II.

38 PRIETO LASA – *Las Leyendas de los Señores
de Vizcaya*, p. 33, 45, 55-6.

interpretations of these tales, such as those by the Portuguese author and ambassador in Rome Félix Machado da Silva Castro e Vasconcelos, the Marquis of Montebelo, given in comments made to the Faria y Sousa edition of the *Book of Lineages*. Félix Machado, along with scolding Labaña for having censured the two tales, further attempts to 'naturalize' their fantastical aspects by claiming these possibly emerged from simple errors originating from oral transmissions, and that such fairies were likely just regular women with natural physical defects.[39]

Condemnatory interpretations of the Goat-Foot tale can also be found, such as those by Diego de Yepes, an obscure character who was likely the chaplain of the Hospital de la Santa Cruz in Toledo, alive during the sixteenth and seventeenth century, and who is also present in several Castilian versions of the *Book of Lineages*. Contrary to Félix Machado's naturalization of Goat-Foot, the purpose of Yepes was

---

39 PRIETO LASA – *Las Leyendas de los Señores de Vizcaya*, p. 66-8.

to highlight the historical veracity of the Goat-Foot tale and portray her as a demonic and satanic agent.[40] Similar are the mentions of the Goat-Foot tale by the Castilian Jesuit Juan Eusebio Nieremberg in his *Cvriosa y Ocvlta Filosofia* (1630), where she is directly referred to as a/the d/Devil and her children likely only illusory.[41]

This construction of Goat-Foot as an explicitly diabolical agent seems to be at the base of a later oral narrative for the lineage of the Castilian Manriques, a version of which was included in some editions of Diego Hernández de Mendoza's already mentioned *Nobiliario*.[42] The version offered by Hernández de Mendoza is a clear derivative of the Haro narrative, describing how the founder of the Manriques was seduced by a/the d/Devil in the form of a beautiful woman. She eventually fled

---

40 PRIETO LASA – *Las Leyendas de los Señores de Vizcaya*, p. 69-71.

41 NIEREMBERG – *Cvriosa y Oculta Filosofia*, p. 97.

42 PRIETO LASA – *Las Leyendas de los Señores de Vizcaya*, p. 167.

when forced to witness the eucharist; when attempting to take their children with her, she dropped one who clefted his foot in the fall.[43]

Even with such occasional negative interpretations, Juan Arranzadi proposes that, given the development of Biscayan lordship rights in the sixteenth century, the popularity of the Goat-Foot narrative was likely taken by the locals to retcon history with the idea that Biscayan lords had traditionally vowed their *fueros* (legislative codes defining and ensuring local regional rights) while having one of their feet bare,[44] as exemplified by Andres Poza in his 1587 *Del la Antigva Lengva, Poplaciones, y Comarcas de las Españas*.[45]

Adding further variability to the body of Iberian fairy women literature, in 1489 the Melusine narrative was translated into Castilian by Juan Parix

---

43 PRIETO LASA – 'Los Manriques,' p. 132-3; BNE, MSS/18244 V.1, fol.152r-155r.

44 ARANZADI – *Milenarismo Vasco*, p. 368.

45 POÇA – *Del la Antigva Lengva, Poplaciones, y Comarcas de las Españas*, fol.50r-53v.

and Esteban Clebat and published in Toulouse as *Historia de la Linda Melosina*[46] (with a Sevillan republication in 1526 and a second translation happening in 1512 in Valencia, of which no copies are known).[47] This new Castilian version of the tale has an uncertain origin, and while it follows the Jean d'Arras *Melusine* story, it is also possible that it was produced from the 1473/4 Bernhard Richel German translation of d'Arras as published in Lyon between 1479 and 1487.[48] Like the narratives of Goat-Foot and Dona Marinha, this Castilian publication cannot be excluded from the political reality of its time. The change from *Melusine* into *Melosina* was not solely a passive translation, but a partial reformulation of this text to cater to the newly established rule of the Catholic Monarchs Fernando of Aragon

---

46 CASAS AGUILAR – 'Architecture and Empire in *Historia de la Linda Melosina*,' p. 109, 111.

47 PRUD'HOMME – 'Mermaid, Mother, Monster, and More,' p. 53.

48 ZELDENRUST – 'Serpent or Half-Serpent?,' p. 24, 28.

and Isabella I of Castile. In particular, this publication seems to serve the purpose of providing its Castilian and Aragonese readers a parallel between Melosina and Isabella I as a way of promoting an image of female power and authority, a trend which is common during the reign of the Catholic Monarchs.[49] Melosina is a figure of female courtly governance, associated with an ideology of territorial and religious expansion, large-scale construction, and imperial and chivalrous ideals.[50]

In more recent times, particular among the developments of the Goat-Foot narrative, and likely the instance which cements this tale in the Portuguese-speaking imaginary, is the adaptation made by the historian and medievalist Alexandre Herculano (1810-1877), originally published in the periodical *O Panorama* in 1843, but mostly known for its inclusion in the second vol-

---

49 CASAS AGUILAR – 'Architecture and Empire in *Historia de la Linda Melosina*,' p. 110.

50 CASAS AGUILAR – 'Architecture and Empire in *Historia de la Linda Melosina*,' p. 111, 115.

ume of his *Lendas e Narrativas* in 1851.[51]
This new version is likely its most popular form and from where the title 'Lady
Goat-Foot' originates. Besides including a
variety of new characters and side plots,
Herculano also reframes Goat-Foot not
so much as a fairy but as the condemned
soul of an adulterous countess. Overall,
the Herculano version has a much greater
alignment with Christian morality, making
Goat-Foot's diabolical association explicit
through various means, such as giving her
two goat feet, instead of the original one.

These changes need to be understood
to have been deliberate, as Herculano
also published the first printed edition
of Pedro Afonso's *Book of Lineages* in the
contemporary period, in which he included
the integral Haro tale. This version of the
Book of Lineages should be further noted for
having been translated into Castilian by
Marcelino Menéndez Pelayo in the late

---

51 PRIETO LASA – *Las Leyendas de los Señores
de Vizcaya*, p. 94; A summary of the Herculano
version is given in LEITÃO – *The Book of St.
Cyprian*, p. 274-5.

nineteenth and early twentieth century, being, together with a twentieth-century translation of the tale by Julio Caro Baroja, a fundamental source for subsequent Spanish academic studies on Biscayan/ Basque mythology, as well as compilations of legends and tales for children.[52]

Not long after the publication of *Lendas e Narrativas*, in 1878 the New York-born Frederico Francisco Stuart de Figanière e Morão (1827-1908), a colleague of Herculano, the Viscount of Figanière and 'late envoy extraordinary and minister plenipotentiary of his Majesty the King of Portugal at the Imperial Court of Russia from 1870 and 1876', published an English-language version of the Goat-Foot tale in verse, entitled *Elva: A Story of the Dark Ages*. Besides his political duties, Figanière was an orientalist, evolutionist, one of the early Portuguese proponents of economic

---

52 PRIETO LASA – *Las Leyendas de los Señores de Vizcaya*, p. 115-6.

liberalism,[53] as well as a known theosophist. His association with the Theosophical Society has, unfortunately, given rise to various stories regarding him and his time in Russia, with several Theosophical sources mentioning that Figanière was a personal acquaintance of Helena Petrova Blavatsky. While such stories are known to already be in circulation in 1921, as stated by the Spanish theosophist Mario Roso de Luna in his *En el Umbral del Misterio: Ciencia y Teosofía*[54] (curiously, this book is prefaced by Enediel Shaiah, or Alfredo Rodríguez Aldao, creator and compiler of the Spanish *El Libro Magno de San Cipriano*, as well as publisher and translator of several other grimoires and occult works),[55] none of these offer any evidence or historically locatable references for this claim, although Figanière was likely to have

---

53 See MACHADO and MESQUITA – 'Um Pioneiro do Liberalismo Económico em Portugal'.

54 ROSO DE LUNA – *En el Umbral del Misterio*, p. 321.

55 CASTRO VICENTE – 'O Libro de San Cibrán,' p. 93-4.

become a member of the London branch
of the Theosophical Society sometime
before 1888.[56]

Even still, Figanière was a known
collaborator of occult periodicals such as
The Aquarian Theosophist, *Light*, *Lucifer* and
The Theosophist, either under his name or
a variety of pseudonyms (some of which
are likely still unknown),[57] with at least
one of his writings in this last periodical
being directly quoted in Blavatsky's *The
Secret Doctrine*.[58] Apart from these works,
he was a writer of supernatural-themed
historically-inspired short stories, with
Elva being a particularly shining example

56 GOMES – *Gnose e Liberdade*, p. 5, 22, 9.

57 CURADO – 'O Pensamento Esotérico do
Visconde de Figanière,' p. 58.

58 BLAVATSKY – *The Secret Doctrine*, vol.
2, p. 302. For an overview of Figanière's
esoteric thinking as expounded on his occultist
*magnum opus Estudos Esotericos: Submundo,
Mundo, Supramundo*, as well as some old-school
uncut theosophical racism, see CURADO –
'O Pensamento Esotérico do Visconde de
Figanière', and ROSO DE LUNA – *En el
Umbral del Misterio*, p. 321-355.

of this line of his work.[59]

Analyzing *Elva* in detail reveals little in the way of explicit references to theosophy or the works of Blavatsky; throughout it Figanière presents himself as considerably informed on English demonological treatises of the early modern period, particularly with James I's *Daemonologie* (1597) and, much more relevantly, with Reginal Scot's *The Discoverie of Witchcraft* (1584),[60] books which he also alludes to in his *Estudos Esotericos*.[61] From within this magical/demonological context, *Elva* explicitly places the character of Goat-Foot in a learned spirit hierarchy, opening with the lines:

> In days when Zimimar was King
> Of all Demons north;
> When Gorson's sultry voice could bring
> The southern dragons forth;
> When Goap on wicked errands sent

---

59 CURADO – 'O Pensamento Esotérico do Visconde de Figanière,' p. 57.

60 FIGANIÉRE – *Elva*, p. 179, 191.

61 ROSO DE LUNA – *En el Umbral del Misterio*, p. 347.

His imps throughout the west;
And the dark fiends of Orient
Obeyed Amaimon's hest;[62]

This is a direct borrowing from Scot's
description of the four kings as "Amaymon
king of the east, Gorson king of the south,
Zimimar king of the north, Goap king and
prince of the west".[63]

Regarding its central character, Figanière portrays Goat-Foot, referred to here
as the titular Elva and later referred to as
Cloven-Foot, as the daughter of a count,
an element he derived from Herculano.
However, in this version, instead of being
a spirit, Elva acquired her supernatural
aspect due to being taken by Goap, king
of the west, who turns her into one of his
sprites and gives her ample knowledge of
herbs,[64] this as a result of a pact made between Elva's father, Laredo, and the spirit
Topel, an envoy of Goap and the son of a

---

62 FIGANIÉRE – *Elva*, p. 1.

63 SCOT – *The Discouerie of Witchcraft*, p. 393.

64 FIGANIÉRE – *Elva*, p. 147.

'Moorish hag' and a 'Jew':[65]

> Its arms were webbed like wings of bat,
> Its legs were bent like those of cat,
> With spring as tensile and as light.
> Measure an ape, you'll have its height.
> The face was that of whiskered owl,
> And fiendish grim was blent with scowl,
> Which nought but mischief dire for-
> bode.
> Body it had of loathsome toad,
> Of dingy colour, flecked with woad.
> Its paunch was creased like moistened
> bladder
> For tail it had a wriggling adder.[66]

This, much like Herculano's version, greatly distances Goat-Foot from her medieval or potentially pre-medieval roots, instead inserting her into a more 'normalized' magical tradition, as besides Scot's *The Discoverie of Witchcraft*, Goap can also be found in several grimoires under the names

---

65 FIGANIÉRE – *Elva*, p. 17.
66 FIGANIÉRE – *Elva*, p. 14

of Gaap, Tap, or Taob, making Goat-Foot
a grimoire spirit by association.[67]

1863 ILLUSTRATION OF GAAP BY LOUIS
LE BRETON FOR COLLIN DE PLANCY'S
DICTIONNAIRE INFERNAL.

---

67 RANKINE – *The Grimoire Encyclopaedia*, vol.
1, p. 441.

Arriving at the twentieth century, both the Goat-Foot and Dona Marinha tales seem to attract the attention of a number of Portuguese mythographers, such as the esotericist and mystical philosopher Dalila Pereira da Costa. During the 1970s and 80s she expounded considerably upon Goat-Foot and Dona Marinha in her writings, placing these side by side in a kind of earth-water spirit duality. In her usual and highly speculative approach,[68] Costa largely reads these tales as expressions of an archaic Great-Mother cult present within Portuguese culture, with Goat-Foot and Marinha being two of her "superior avatars", with shamanic overtones.[69] Also, the earth-water duality Costa constructs is presented as a form of historical 'premonition' pointing towards the fulfillment of a Portuguese spiritual vocation in the kingdom's maritime expansion given the benefic and conciliatory conclusion of the Marinha

---

68 Euphemism.

69 COSTA – *Da Serpente à Imaculada*, p. 86, 326; COSTA – *A Ladainha de Setúbal*, p. 112.

tale… and something about Atlantis too.[70] As a historian of magic and religion it is not my place to judge appropriations of symbols and narratives into new forms of spirituality, but what a politically motivated Biscayan adaptation of a melusinian-tale and its ironic flip by a disgruntled Galician admiral later used by immigrant knights seeking social acceptance has to do with Portuguese manifest destiny and archaic spirituality is anyone's guess.

Turning back the clock, the recently departed medieval historian José Mattoso returned these two tales to their medieval form by publishing a critical edition of Pedro Afonso's *Book of Lineages* in 1980, with partial republications of this work having been done in 1983 and 2020.[71] This 1980 edition has given rise to an increased visibility and academic interest in not only the *Book of Lineages* but also in these two

---

70 COSTA – *A Ladainha de Setúbal*, p. 116-7, 139-40.

71 See MATTOSO – 'Livro de Linhagens do Conde D. Pedro' and MATTOSO – *Narrativas dos Livros de Linhagens*.

tales in particular, with ample scholarly
publications currently available. Yet,
within the consciousness of the general
public Herculano's version remains
dominant and is currently the source of
new adaptations and repurposings of the
character of Goat-Foot in various forms of
media, both in Portugal and Brazil.[72]

Finally, and veering once again into
explicitly magical realms, one of the most
interesting and unexpected references to
Goat-Foot can be found in the Cyprianic
grimoire referred to as *Heptameron: Ó
Elementos Mágicos*. In the wider context
of Cyprianic magic literature, this book
stands rather isolated as one of the very
few Iberian Cyprian texts which does not

---

72 See SANTOS, ANDRADE, NEDBAJLUK
and ZLATIC – 'A Leitura da Dama do Pé
de Cabra na Perspectiva das Novas Mídias
Digitais'.

contain the Prayer of Saint Cyprian;[73] the only mention it makes of the sorcerer saint of Antioch and Iberian magic-hero is on its cover page. While its original publication date is unknown, the researcher Félix Castro Vicente marks this as, potentially, one of the oldest printed Books of Saint Cyprian, perhaps dating from 1810 (prior to the Herculano version of the Goat-Foot tale).[74]

---

73 A talismanic magico-religious text part of a wider 'Western' magico-religious arsenal, used as a method for the banishment of evil spirits, sorcery, and the evil eye, known in regions as varied as Italy, Scandinavia, and the Arabic world, and extremely popular in Iberia. In particular, this text can be seen to stand at the center of the early modern creation of the Iberian grimoire tradition of the Books of Saint Cyprian. DUNI – 'Esorcisti o Stregoni?,' p. 273; BJÖRN GÅRDBÄCK – 'Cyprianus Förmaning,' p. 36–50; BASSET – *Les Apocryphes Éthiopiens*, p. 6-24, p. 38-52; PAIVA – *Bruxaria e Superstição*, p. 110, 116.

74 CASTRO VICENTE – 'O Libro de San Cibrán,' p. 88.

HEPTAMERON

ó

ELEMENTOS MAGICOS

COMPUESTO POR EL GRAN **CIPRIANO** FAMOSO
MAJICO, TRADUCIDO AL LATIN Y DE ESTE AL
FRANCES.

POR ESTERHAAZY

Y ULTIMAMENTE A LA LENGUA CASTELLANA,

POR FABIO SALAZAR Y QUINCOCES.

ASCROLOGO, ALQUIMISLA Y PROFUNDO
NATURALISTA.

VENECIA.
Imprenta y Librería de Francesco Succoni.
Año de M.DCCXXII.

COVER OF THE CYPRIANIC HEPTAMERON: Ó
ELEMENTOS MAGICOS.

The *Heptameron* is a short text (about 90 pages), much of it is focused on issues of divination, containing an extended section dedicated to what it refers to as 'Astrological Chyromancy'. This section is difficult to fully comprehend, making several overlaps between chiromancy proper, astrology, and apparent zodiacal spirits and their sigils. These spirits, while having some potential international grimoiric correspondences, such as with the already mentioned four kings or six elemental rulers, also bear recurrent relations to local Iberian folklore, mentioning *duendes*, *follets*, and possibly *xanas*.[75] One of these spirits in particular, associated with the sign of Gemini, is offered in the *Heptameron*'s list of dark/black genii as *Pie de Ciervo*, or Deer Foot:

> To the same constellation [Gemini]
> belongs Deer Foot queen of incu-
> bi. She appears under the figure of
> a beautiful woman but hiding her
> deer foot under her long dress. She

75 STRATTON-KENT – *The Testament of Cyprian the Mage*, vol. 2, p. 178.

protects hunters, but she exposes
them to filthy/illicit loves/delights.
Bad star.[76]

The association of Deer Foot with
Goat-Foot seems rather direct, not
only due to their similar names and the
extreme closeness of their overall physical
description, but also due to the reference
to Deer Foot as queen of incubi. While
fairly unknown, and of considerably
difficult interpretation, the very last
section of the Goat-Foot tale from the
Book of Lineages, which is very rarely
included in subsequent publications of the

---

76 'A la misma constelacio pertenece Pie
de ciervo reina de los íncubos. Aparece
bajo la figura de una mujer hermosa pera
escondiendo bajo su largo traje un pié de
ciervo. Protejer los cazadores pero los espone á
los amores inmundos. Mala estrella,' in Anon.
– *Heptameron*, p. 28.

story,[77] has her transform into a serpent
to which tribute is occasionally given by
Biscayan lords. Eventually, due to another
breaking of a taboo, this serpent is said
to have started acting in an incubus-like
manner, attacking Biscayan village girls 'as
a squire', forcefully lying with them and
leaving them drained or pale.

Falling back on the Goat-Foot/Mari
relation, as pointed out by José Ramón
Prieto Lasa, Basque translations of this
particular section of Pedro Afonso's *Book
of Lineages* explicitly refer to this serpent
as *Anbotoko Mari* or *Anbotoko sorgiña* (Mari
or sorcerer of Amboto).[78] Furthermore
this serpent can be interpreted as Maju
or Sugaar/Zugaar, the male counterpart
of Mari, described as a fiery male serpent

77 This not being included in the seventeenth
century Bautista Labaña and Faria y Sousa
versions, ignored in the romanticized
Herculano version and partially censured from
Figanière's notes on *Elva*; FIGANIÉRE – *Elva*,
p. 194; PRIETO LASA – *Las Leyendas de los
Señores de Vizcaya*, p. 10.

78 PRIETO LASA – *Las Leyendas de los Señores
de Vizcaya*, p. 120.

who joins with her on Fridays and whose
sexual congress generates storms and
hail.[79] What is potentially suggested is that
this duality is united in Pedro Afonso's
version of the Goat-Foot narrative, with
this being Mari and Sugaar simultaneously
or these two forces being manifested within
the same character at different stages of
its interaction and relationship with the
Biscayan lords.

Another connection which can be
made is through the work of Lope Garcia
Salazar, a fifteenth century Biscayan historian. Writing around one century after
Pedro Afonso, Garcia Salazar offers an
alternative lineage of the Biscayan lords
in his *Crónica de Siete Casas de Vizcaya y Cas-
tilla* (1454), omitting the Goat-Foot narrative but initiating it with the tale of an
unnamed Scottish princess who arrived
in Biscay (similar to Froom from the Pedro Afonso lineage), and there laid with 'a
devil which in Biscayan is called Culebro

79 ARANZADI – *Milenarismo Vasco*, p. 339.

[Serpent], Lord of the House',[80] giving
birth to Jaun Zuría, first lord of Biscay.
This narrative, besides also resembling Antonio Torquemada's alternative Marinho
foundation narrative, seems to once again
borrow Arthurian elements, namely by its
similarity to the birth of Merlin, which
Garcia Salazar includes in his *Libro de las
Bienandanzas e Fortunas* (1471-1476). In this
Merlin is mentioned as being fathered by
the devil Ynquibides (incubus).[81]

Both the end of the Pedro Afonso
narrative and the beginning of the Garcia
Salazar narrative thus address the same
apparent idea of a Biscayan supernatural
serpent taking sexual advantage of local
girls. This, from a Basque perspective,
would fit the role of Sugaar or a more
complex Mari-Maju idea which both
edifies and destroys local lordship
authority and descendance. Whoever

---

80 'un diablo que llaman en Bizcaya Culebro,
Senor de Casa,' in ARANZADI – *Milenarismo
Vasco*, p. 356.

81 JUARISTI – 'Los Mitos de Origen en la
Génesis de las Identidades Nacionales', p. 211.

the author of the Cyprianic *Heptameron*
might have been, in this one point he
thus demonstrates considerable awareness
of the nuances and variations of Basque
and Biscayan mythology, and besides all
the previous considerations—even if this
cannot be much more than speculation—
the characteristics of both Mari and
Maju/Sugaar present in this entry might
also be the reason why Deer Foot was placed
as a spirit of Gemini. Throughout all of
this, and more efficiently than Figanière,
the Cyprian *Heptameron* appears to elevate
Goat-Foot from more than a genealogical
tool for noblilistic powerplays, endowing
her with a certain degree of autonomy and
independence as a fully-fledged Iberian
grimoire spirit.

Furthermore, it should be noted that
Melusina is also listed in the Cyprianic
Heptameron as a spirit associated with Aries.
By the description given, it is clear this is not
one of her Iberian variations, such as Lady
Marinha, who, apart from the occasional
compilation of Portuguese legends, has
not made much of a contemporary
mark. However, given the *Heptameron*'s

particular spelling of this name (Melusina, as opposed to Melusine), it cannot be said that this is the French fairy either, and a point can be made that this is a reference to her Castilian adaptation as published in the fifteenth century: the empire builder *Linda Melosina*:

> To the constellation [Aries] belongs the house of *Melusina*, who every Saturday is covered with scales from the waist down to the tips of her feet. This is a lover of mysterious, discrete people, and she teaches one how to keep a secret. Good star.[82]

Taken by the Cyprianic *Heptameron*, the late, great Jake Stratton-Kent would relate the mention to Deer Foot to the Native American figure of Deer Woman, proposing a possible overlap of European

---

82 'Pertenece á la misma constelación la casa de *Melusina*, que todos los sábados se cubre de escamas desde la cintura hasta la estremidad de los pies. Es amante de las personas misteriosas, discretas y enseña á saber guardar un secreto. Buena estrella,' in Anon. – *Heptameron*, p. 27.

and American mythical figures in this reference.[83] This hypothesis is somewhat of a stretch, but while proposing it, Jake does admit that '[p]ossibly there is also an Iberian figure I have overlooked'.

Yes there is and yes you did Jake. Wish we had the opportunity to talk about it.

*

What follows is the translation of the José Mattoso transcriptions of the Biscayan Haro and Galician Marinho melusinian-tales from the *Book of Lineages of Count Dom Pedro*. Certain structural, grammatical and punctuation aspects of the original texts were altered, both to make these closer to contemporary English-language standards and for purposes of clarity.

---

83 STRATTON-KENT – *The Testament of Cyprian the Mage*, vol. 2, p. 179-80.

Lady Goat-Foot

Dom Diego Lopez was a very good rider. One day, when he was out with his company searching for a boar, he heard the loud singing of a woman from atop a cliff. He went there and saw that she was very beautiful and well-dressed, and was greatly enamored by her, and asked who she was.

She told him she was a woman of very great lineage, and he replied that if she was a woman of very great lineage, he would wed her, should she wish, as he was the lord of that whole land. She told him she would, should he promise to never bless himself. He thus granted, and she went with him.

This lady was greatly beautiful and very well composed of body, save that she had a forked foot, such as a goat's foot. And they lived a great many years [together], and had two children, one with the name of Enheguez Guerra and the other, a woman, had the name of ___.

When they ate, Dom Diego Lopez and
his wife, he would sit his son to his side,
and she the daughter to the other side.
One day he went to his lands and killed
a great boar and brought it home and
placed it before himself and thus he ate it
with his wife and their children. He cast a
bone from the table, and an alaunt and a
warren came to fight over it, in such a way
that the warren took to the alaunt by the
throat and killed it.

Dom Diego Lopez, when he saw this,
took it for a miracle, and blessed himself
and said: "Holy Mary [be] praised, never
such a thing was seen!"

His wife, when she saw him thus bless
himself, cast a hand on the daughter and
the son. Dom Diego Lopes stopped that of
the son, and did not want to let her take
him, so she took the daughter through a
window of the palace, and went to the
mountains, in such a way that she was
never again seen, nor was the daughter.

After some time, this Dom Diego Lopez
went to do harm to the Moors, and these
arrested him and took him to Toledo to be
imprisoned. This imprisonment weighed

upon his son Enheguez Guerra, and he
came to speak with those of that land about
a way to take him [Dom Diego Lopez] out
of prison. They told him they knew of no
way he could have him, save if he went to
the mountains and found his mother; she
would give him the way of getting him out.
Thus he went, on his horse, and found her
atop a cliff.

She said to him: "Son, Enheguez
Guerra, come to me for I know what you
come for." And he went to her and she told
him: "You come to ask how to take your
father from prison."

Then she called a horse that wandered
loose on the mount, and was called Pardalo,
and she called him by his name. And she
put a bridle on the horse, which she had,
and told him [Enheguez Guerra] not to
force on him the saddle, nor the bridle, nor
give him food, nor drink, nor horseshoes;
she told him this horse would last his entire
life, that he would never enter battle with it
and not win. And she told him to ride the
horse and that it would take him to Toledo,
before the door where his father was, that
very day, and that … there he should get

off and find his father in a corral, and grab him by the hand and make as though he wanted to speak with him, and thus bring him [back] to the door where the horse was. As long as it happened in this way – that he rode the horse with his father placed before him – before nightfall he would be in his own lands with his father. And this was so.

After some time, Dom Diego Lopez died, and the land was left to his son Enheguez Guerra. There are some in Biscay who said and say today of the mother of Enheguez Guerra, that this is the serpent of Biscay. Each who is a lord of Biscay, in a village they call Vusturio, of the bellies of the cows they kill, they order a piece to be placed outside of the village, on a cliff; in the morning they do not find it nor anything. They say that if they do not do so they will receive some spite from [the serpent] on that day and night, on some squire or their house, or on some other thing which would pain them. This was always held in this way by the lords of Biscay until the death of Dom Joham, the Crooked. Some wanted to test [this] by not doing it, and they had it badly. They

further say that today, this [serpent] comes
to lie with some women in the villages, even
if they do not want it. It come to them as
a squire, all of those who are laid become
drained.

Lady Marinha

The first [of this line] was a very good knight who had the name of Froiam, and he was a hunter and rider. One day while on his horse, above the sea, on his hunt, he found a beautiful sea woman lying sleeping in the creek. Three of his squires went with him. She, when she felt them, wanted to take to the sea, but they went in such a way after her [that] they captured her before she could escape. And after they had captured her, he [Froiam] made them place her over a beast, and he took her to his home.

She was very beautiful and he had her baptized. No other name fitted her such as Marinha, for she had come from the sea; thus he named her, and they called her, Lady Marinha. He had from her his sons, of whom one was named Joham Frioaz Marinho.

This Lady Marinha did not speak even a crumb. Dom Friam loved her greatly

and never did he not do all the things he
could to make her speak. One day he had
a great fire made in his palace, and as she
was coming in from outside with that son
of hers, whom she loved as her heart, Dom
Froia[m] grabbed that son of his and hers,
and made as if wanting to cast him into the
fire. She, with rage over the son, made to
shout, and with her shout she cast a piece
of flesh from her mouth, and from then
onward she spoke. Dom Froia[m] received
her as a wife and married her.

Bibliography

Anon. – *Heptameron: Ó Elementos Magicos Compuesto Por el Gran Cipriano Famoso Majico, Traducido el Latin y de Este al Frances por Esterhaazy y Ultimamente e la Lengua Castellana, Por Fabio Salazar y Quincoces, Astrologo, Alquimisla e Profundo Naturalista.* Barcelona: Parsival Ediciones, 1989.

Arquivo Nacional da Torre de Tombo (ANTT), Livros de Linhagens, Nobiliário de Espanha Escrito pelo Senhor Conde D. Pedro.

Arquivo Nacional da Torre do Tombo (ANTT), Tribunal do Santo Ofício, Inquisição de Lisboa, Processos, nº5605, *Processo de Maria Gonçalves*, 1627–1630.

Biblioteca Nacional de España (BNE), MSS/18244 V.1, MSS/18245 V.2, HERNÁNDEZ DE MANDONZA, Deigo - El Becerro General: Libro en que se Relata el Blasón de las Armas que Trahen Muchos Reynos y Imperios, Señoríos y la Causa porque

y Dotuvieron su Principio; y de la
Genealogía de los Lynages de España,
y de los Escudos de Armas que Trahen.

COSTA, Dalila L. Pereira da – *A Ladainha de Setúbal: E o Eremita da Arrábida*. Lello & Irmão – Editores, 1989.

COSTA, Dalila L. Pereira da – *Da Serpente à Imaculada*. Porto: Livraria Chardron de Lello & Irmão – Editores, 1984.

FIGANIÉRE, Viscount de – *Elva: A Story of the Dark Ages*. London: Trübner & Co., 1878.

HERCULANO, Alexandre – *Lendas e Narrativas*. Lisbon: Casa da Viuva Bertrand e Filhos, 2 vols., 1858-1859.

MATTOSO, José – 'Livro de Linhagens do Conde D. Pedro (Critical Edition)'. *Portvgaliæ Monvmenta Historica: A Sæcvlo Octavo post Christvm Vsqve ad Qvintvmdecimvm Ivssv Academiæ Scientiarvm Olisiponensis Edita (Nova Série)*, vol.2, part 1-2 (1980) p.7-493, 9-397.

MATTOSO, José – *Narrativas dos Livros de Linhagens*. Lisbon: Círculo de Leitores, Temas e Debates, 2020.

NIEREMBERG, Ivan Evsevio – *Cvriosa y Ocvlta Filosofía: Primera, y Segvnda Parte de las Maravillas de la Naturaleza, Examinadas en Varias Questiones Naturales. Continene Historias Mvy Notables. Averiganse Secretos, y Problemas de la Naturaleza con Filosofía Nueva, Explicanse Lugares Dificultoso de Escritura. Obra Muy Util, no Solo para los Curiosos, Sino para Doctores Escriturarios, Filósofos, y Medicos*. Madrid: Imprenta Real, 1649.

PIEL, Joseph and MATTOSO, José – 'Livros Velhos de Linhagens (Critical Edition)'. *Portvgaliæ Monvmenta Historica: A Sæcvlo Octavo post Christvm Vsqve ad Qvintvmdecimvm Ivssv Academiæ Scientiarvm Olisiponensis Edita (Nova Série)*, vol.1 (1980), p. 9-368.

SCOT, Reginald – *The Discouerie of Witchcraft, Wherein the Lewde Dealing of Witches and Witchmongers is Notablie Detected, the Knauerei of Coniurors, the Impieti of Inchantors, the Follie of Soothsaiers, the Impudent Falshood of Cousenors, the Infidelitie of Atheists, the Pestilent Practises of Pythonists, the Curiosities of Figurecasters, the Vanities of Dreamers, the Beggerlie of Alcumystrie, the Abhomination of Idolatrie, the Horrible Art of Poisoning, the Vertue and Power of Naturall Magike, and All the Conueiances of Legierdemain and Iuggling are Deciphered and Many Other Things Opened, Which Have Long Lien Hidden, Howbeit Verie Necessarie to be Knowne. Herevnto is Added a Treatise vpon the Nature and Substance of Spirits and Devils, &c.* London: William Brome, 1584.

TORQUEMADA, Antonio – *Iardin de Flores Cvriosas, en que se Tratan Algvnas Materias de Hvmanidad, Philosophia, Theologia, y Geographia, con Otras Cosas Curiosas, y Apazibles.* Antwerp: Iuan Corderio, 1575.

SECONDARY SOURCES:

ARANZADI, Juan – 'Mari, Melusina y los Origenes Miticos de los Señores de Vizcaya'. *Los Cuadernos del Norte: Revista cultural de la Caja de Ahorros de Asturias*, 5 (1981) p. 2-8.

ARANZADI, Juan – *Milenarismo Vasco: Edad de Oro, Etnia y Nativismo.* Madrid: Tauros, 2000.

BAIN, Frederika – 'The Tail of Melusine: Hybridity, Mutability, and the Accessible Other,' in URBAN, Misty, KEMMIS, Deva F. and ELMES, Melissa Ridley (eds.) – *Melusine's Footprint: Tracing the Legacy of a Medieval Myth*. Leiden; Boston: Brill, 2017, p. 17-35.

BASSET, René – *Les Apocryphes Éthiopiens – IV: Les Prières de S. Cyprien et de Théophile*. Milan: Archè, 1982.

BJÖRN GÅRDBÄCK, Johannes – 'Cyprianus Förmaning,' in CUMMINS, Alexander, HATHAWAY DIAZ, Jesse and ZAHRT, Jennifer (eds.) – *Cypriana: Old World*. Seattle: Revelore Press, 2017, p. 36–50.

BLAVATSKY, H. P. – *The Secret Doctrine: The Synthesis of Science, Religion, and Philosophy*. London: The Theosophical Publishing House, 2 vols., 1893.

CARDIGOS, Isabel – '«Dona Marinha»: Uma Figura Melusínica?,' in NOIA, Camiño (ed.) – *Imaxes de Muller: Representación da Feminidade en Mitos, Contos e Lendas*. Vigo: Universidade de Vigo, 2012, p. 73-81.

CARO BAROJA, Julio – *Algunos Mitos*

Españoles y Otros Ensayos. Madrid: Editora Nacional, 1944.

CARO, Rodrigo – *Días Geniales ó Lúdicros*. Seville: Imp. De El Mercantil Sevillano, 1884.

CASAS AGUILAR, Anna – 'Architecture and Empire in *Historia de la Linda Melosina*,' in URBAN, Misty, KEMMIS, Deva F. and ELMES, Melissa Ridley (eds.) – *Melusine's Footprint: Tracing the Legacy of a Medieval Myth*. Leiden; Boston: Brill, 2017, p. 109-131.

CASTRO VICENTE, Félix Francisco – 'O Libro de San Cibrán: Unha Realidade no Imaxinario Popular'. *Murguía: Revista Galega de Historia*, 12 (2007) p. 69-104.

CONSTANZA CERUTI, María – 'Montañas Sagradas en el País Vasco e su Mitologia'. *Mitológicas*, 26 (2011) p. 29-42.

CURADO, Manuel – 'O Pensamento Esotérico do Visconde de Figanière (1827-1908),' in ÁLVARES, Cristina, CURADO, Ana Lúcia, SOUSA, Sérgio Guimarães de and MATEUS, Isabel Cristina – *O Imaginário Esotérico: Literatura Cinema Banda Desenhada*. Famalicão:

Centro de Estudos Humanísticos da Universidade do Minho; Edições Húmus, 2016, p. 57-75.

DUNI, Matteo – 'Esorcisti o Stregoni? Identità Professionale del Clero e Inquisizione a Modena nel Primo Cinquecento'. *Mélanges de l'Ecole Française de Rome, Italie et Méditerranée*, 115:1 (2003) p. 263-85.

FERREIRA, Maria do Rosário – '«Amor e Amizade Antre os Nobres Fidalgos de Espanha»: Apontamentos Sobre o Prólogo do *Livro de Linhagens* do Conde D. Pedro'. *Cahiers d'Études Hispaniques Médiévales*, 35 (2012) p. 93-122.

GOMES, Pinharanda – *Gnose e Liberdade: Notas à Obra do Visconde de Figaniére: O Novelista Luso-Brasileiro, o Erudito, o Filósofo, o Personalista*. Braga: Cadernos de Cultura Parábola, 1976.

JUARISTI, Jon – 'Los Mitos de Origen en la Génesis de las Identidades Nacionales: La Batalla de Arrigorriaga y el Surgimiento del Particularismo Vasco (ss. XIV-XVI)'. *Studia Histórica-Historia Contemporánea*, 12 (1994) p. 191-228.

KRUS, Luís – *A Concepção Nobiliárquica do Espaço Ibérico: Geografia dos Livros de Linhagens Medievais Portugueses (1280-1380)*. Lisbon: Faculdade de Ciências Sociais e Humanas da Universidade Nova de Lisboa, 1989 (PhD thesis).

KRUS, Luís – 'A Morte das Fadas: A Lenda Genealógica da Dama do Pé de Cabra'. *Ler História*, 6 (1985) p. 3-34.

LE GOFF, Jacques – 'Mélusine Maternelle et Défricheuse'. *Annales: Economies, Sociétés, Civilisations*, 26:3-4 (1971) p. 587-622.

LECAUTEUX, Claude – 'La Structure des Légendes Mélusiniennes'. *Annales: Economies, Sociétés, Civilisations*, 33:2 (1978) p. 294-306.

LEITÃO, José – *The Book of St. Cyprian: The Sorcerer's Treasure*. France: Hadean Press, 2014.

MACHADO, António Palhinha and MESQUITA, António Pedro – 'Um Pioneiro do Liberalismo Económico em Portugal: Notas de Leitura Sobre a Guerra e o Comércio Livre de Frederico de la Figanière'. Philosophica, 23 (2004) p. 159-165.

MONREAL ZIA, Gregorio (intro.), DOUGLASS, William A. (trans.) and WHITE, Linda (trans.) – *The Old Law of Bizkaia (1452): Introductory Study and Critical Edition*. Reno: Center for Basque Studies; University of Nevada, 2005.

PAIVA, José Pedro – *Bruxaria e Superstição: Num País sem "Caça às Bruxas"*. Lisbon: Editorial Notícias, 2002.

PIZARRO, José Augusto de Sotto Mayor – *D. Dinis*. Maia: Círculo de Leitores, Centro de Estudos dos Povos e Culturas de Expressão Portuguesa, 2020.

POÇA, Andres de – *Del la Antigva Lengva, Poplaciones, y Comarcas de las Españas, en que de Paso se Tocan Algunas Cosas de la Cantabria*. Bilbao: Mathias Mares, 1587.

PRIETO LASA, J. Ramón – *Las Leyendas de los Señores de Vizcaya: y la Tadición Melusiniana*. Madrid: Fundación Ramón Menéndez Pidal; Fundación de la Universidad Autónoma de Madrid; Universidad del País Vasco,1995.

PRIETO LASA, J. Ramón – 'Los Manriques: De Antonio de Trueba al Conde de Barcelos'. *Estudos de Literatura Oral*, 1 (1995) p. 128-143.

PRUD'HOMME, Caroline – 'Mermaid, Mother, Monster, and More: Portraits of the Fairy Woman in Fifteenth- and Sixteenth-Century *Melusine* Narratives,' in URBAN, Misty, KEMMIS, Deva F. and ELMES, Melissa Ridley (eds.) – *Melusine's Footprint: Tracing the Legacy of a Medieval Myth*. Leiden; Boston: Brill, 2017, p. 52-73.

RANKINE, David – *The Grimoire Encyclopaedia*. Keighley: Hadean Press Limited, 2 vols., 2023.

ROSO DE LUNA, Mario – *En el Umbral del Misterio: Ciencia y Teosofía*. Madrid: Editorial Pueyo, 1921.

SANTOS, Amanda Ingrid dos, ANDRADE, Jonabelle de, NEDBAJLUK, Mateus and ZLATIC, Carlos Eduardo – 'A Leitura da Dama do Pé de Cabra na Perspectiva das Novas Mídias Digitais'. *Revista Vernáculo*, 43 (2017) p. 248-277.

STRATTON-KENT, Jake – *The Testament of Cyprian the Mage: Encyclopædia Goetica Volume III, Comprehending the Book of Saint Cyprian & His Magical Elements and the Elucidation of the Testament of Solomon.*

N.p.: Scarlet Imprint, 2 vols., 2014.

TENREIRO BERMÚDEZ, Marcial – 'A Lenda Melusínica no Folclore Galego: Apuntamentos Sobre o Culto e o Popular,' in ROMERO PORTILLA, Paz and GARCÍA HURTADO, Manuel Reyes (eds.) – *De Culturas, Lenguas y Tradiciones: II Simposio de Estudio Humanísitcos*. Coruña: Universidade da Coruña, 2007, p. 263-279.

URBAN, Misty, KEMMIS, Deva F. and ELMES, Melissa Ridley – 'Introduction,' in URBAN, Misty, KEMMIS, Deva F. and ELMES, Melissa Ridley (eds.) – *Melusine's Footprint: Tracing the Legacy of a Medieval Myth*. Leiden; Boston: Brill, 2017, p. 1-13.

ZELDENRUST, Lydia – 'Serpent or Half-Serpent? Berhard Richel's Melusine and the Making of a Western European Icon'. *Neophilologus*, 100 (2016) p. 19-41.

Index

A

B

E

F

G

www.ingramcontent.com/pod-product-compliance
Lightning Source LLC
Chambersburg PA
CBHW051210090426
42740CB00021B/3442